Contents

Sarah's glasses

Sarah wears glasses to read.

My Visit to the Optician

Rachel Tisdale

Photography by Chris Fairclough

W

First published in 2007 by
Franklin Watts
338 Euston Road
London NW1 3BH

Franklin Watts Australia
Level 17/207 Kent Street
Sydney NSW 2000

ISBN: 978 0 7496 7454 0 (hbk)
ISBN: 978 0 7496 7466 3 (pbk)

Dewey classification number: 617.7

A CIP catalogue record for this book is available from the British Library.

Planning and production by Discovery Books Limited
Editor: James Nixon
Designer: Ian Winton
Photography: Chris Fairclough
Series advisors: Diana Bentley MA and Dee Reid MA,
Fellows of Oxford Brookes University

The author, packager and publisher would like to thank the following
people for their participation in this book: Sarah, Jacob, Marcia and Daniel
Hadland; Neil Jones and staff at Specsavers Opticians, Birmingham.

All photographs by Chris Fairclough.

Printed in China

Franklin Watts is a division of Hachette Children's books,
an Hachette Livre UK company.

They help her see
the words.

Eye test

Today Mum takes Sarah to the optician for an eye test.

Sarah remembers
to bring her glasses.

Waiting area

When they arrive they sit in the waiting area.

The optician then calls Sarah into the eye test room.

Letter chart

Sarah looks at
a letter chart.

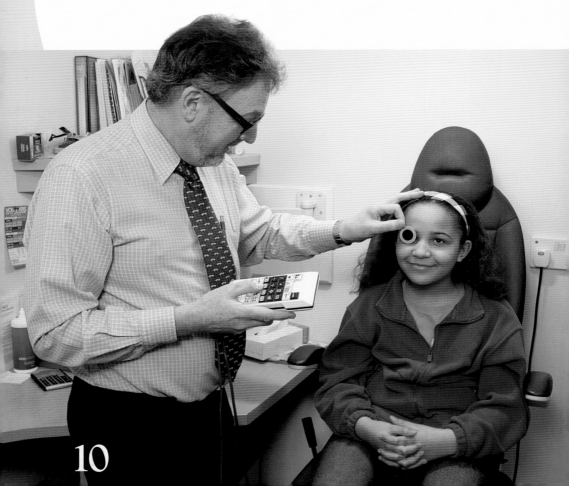

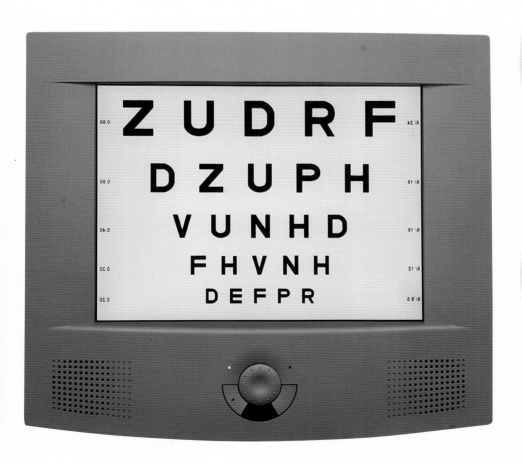

She reads aloud the
letters she can see.

11

Shining light

Next, the optician shines a light into Sarah's eyes.

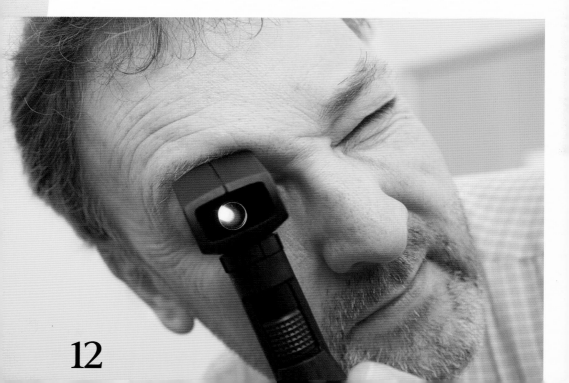

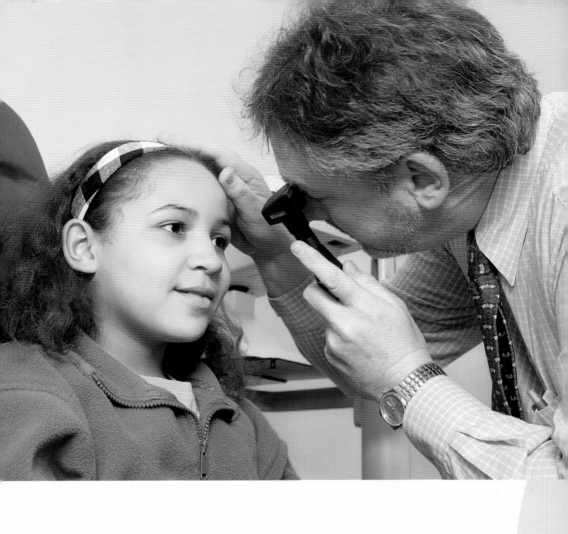

Sarah has to look up,
down, left and right.

Testing lenses

The optician tries lots of different lenses.

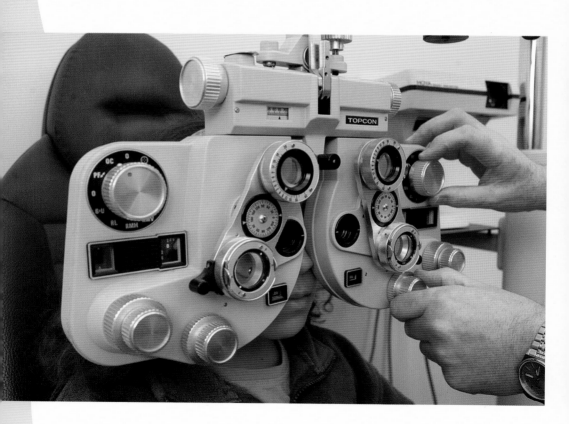

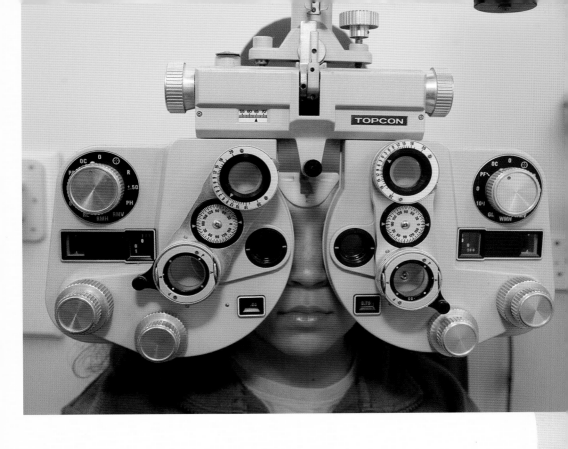

Sarah tells the
optician when
she can see clearly.

New glasses

Sarah needs
new glasses.

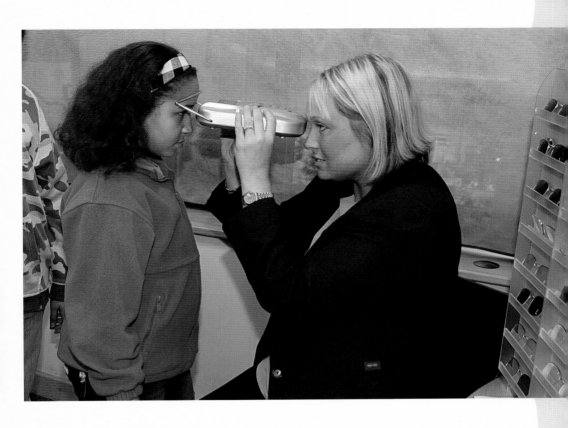

The assistant
measures Sarah
for her new glasses.

Trying on frames

Sarah tries on some new frames.

She likes
the pink
ones best.

11-15 yrs

FREE
GLASSES

1/2 PRICE
SUNGLASSES

19

Making the glasses

The frames are sent to the lab.

They are
fitted
with the
new lenses.

21

Going home

The assistant gives Sarah her new glasses.

Thank you.

Sarah's dad loves her new glasses.

Word bank

Look back for these words and pictures.

Assistant

Frames

Glasses

Lenses

Letter chart

Light

Measures

Optician

Read